GROCERY SHOPPING:
It's In The Bag

Slim Goodbody's
LIGHTEN UP
SERIES

Crabtree Publishing Company
www.crabtreebooks.com

Series Development and Packaging: John Burstein, Slim Goodbody Corp.
Senior Script Development: Phoebe Backler
Managing Editor: Valerie J. Weber
Designer and Illustrator: Ben McGinnis
Graphic Design Agency: Adventure Advertising
Instructional Designer: Alan Backler, Ph. D.
Content Consultant: Betty Hubbard, Ed. D., Certified Health Education Specialist
Project Editor: Reagan Miller

Library and Archives Canada Cataloguing in Publication

Burstein, John.
  Grocery shopping : it's in the bag / Slim Goodbody.

(Slim Goodbody's lighten up!)
ISBN 978-0-7787-3916-6 (bound).--ISBN 978-0-7787-3934-0 (pbk.)

  1. Grocery shopping--Juvenile literature. 2. Nutrition--Juvenile literature. I. Title. II. Series: Goodbody, Slim. Slim Goodbody's lighten up!

TX356.G66 2008   j641.3'1   C2008-900729-8

Library of Congress Cataloging-in-Publication Data

Burstein, John.
  Grocery shopping : it's in the bag / John Burstein.
    p. cm. -- (Slim Goodbody's lighten up!)
  Includes index.
  ISBN-13: 978-0-7787-3916-6 (rlb)
  ISBN-10: 0-7787-3916-3 (rlb)
  ISBN-13: 978-0-7787-3934-0 (pb)
  ISBN-10: 0-7787-3934-1 (pb)
  1. Grocery shopping--Juvenile literature. 2. Nutrition--Juvenile literature. I. Title. II. Series.

TX356.B848 2008
613.2--dc22
                                                    2008003594

Crabtree Publishing Company
www.crabtreebooks.com   1-800-387-7650

Published in Canada
Crabtree Publishing
616 Welland Ave.
St. Catharines, Ontario
L2M 5V6

Published in the United States
Crabtree Publishing
PMB16A
350 Fifth Ave., Suite 3308
New York, NY 10118

Published in the United Kingdom
Crabtree Publishing
White Cross Mills
High Town, Lancaster
LA1 4XS

Published in Australia
Crabtree Publishing
386 Mt. Alexander Rd.
Ascot Vale (Melbourne)
VIC 3032

"Slim Goodbody" and "Lighten Up with Slim Goodbody" are registered trademarks of the Slim Goodbody Corp.

Printed in the U.S.A.

TABLE OF CONTENTS

Slim Goodbody's **LIGHTEN UP** SERIES

HELLO THERE. I'M SLIM GOODBODY,

and my greatest goal in life is to help young people across the planet become healthy and active. After all, one in three kids in the United States is overweight. Without changing their eating and exercise habits, many of these young people will become overweight adults. They risk many possible health problems like **high blood pressure** or **diabetes**.

Today, I would like to introduce you to my friend Mandy. Mandy is known at her high school as a talented artist, and she's hoping to attend art camp this summer. To save enough money for camp, Mandy is working after school at her local grocery store. Join her as she learns about **nutrition** and becoming a smart shopper.

A New Job

Hi! My name is Mandy. I love to paint and create sculptures. I have to save up money this year so I can go to an art camp this summer. Last week, I applied for a job after school working at our local grocery store.

I was happy when I got called in for an interview and even more excited when I was offered the job. The day before I started, I sat at the kitchen table with my mother. "I never really imagined myself bagging groceries and stocking shelves," I said. "I hope I can find ways to make it fun."

Learning for Life

"I think this new job will be great, Mandy. You'll be able to learn a lot about nutrition and making healthy choices when you go grocery shopping. Those are important skills to have if you want to eat a well-balanced diet and grow up into a healthy, energetic adult," said my mother.

"I guess you're right," I said, with a shrug. "It always seems so confusing when I go to the grocery store. There are so many different kinds of foods to choose from. I never know what to buy."

Slim Goodbody Says: The average supermarket has over 40,000 items on its shelves! It can be hard to choose healthy foods with so many options. Learn as much as you can about nutrition to help you decide what's healthiest for you!

"You're never too young to learn how to choose healthy foods, Mandy. Plus, the more you learn about becoming a healthy shopper, the less you'll bug me to buy junk food! Less junk food in the house will help our entire family stay healthier," said my mom.

KNOW YOUR STORE

The next day after school, I walked to the grocery store. I found my supervisor in the back office.

"Hi, Mandy, I'm Ethan," said Ethan with a grin.

"It's nice to meet you," I replied.

"I want to start your training with a tour of the grocery store," said Ethan. "Around the outside of the store, you'll find the healthiest, most natural foods like fruits, vegetables, dairy products, grains, and fresh meat and fish."

EGGS& DAIRY	FRESH MEATS AND SEAFOOD			BAKERY
TOILETRIES AND PAPER PRODUCTS	SODA AND SNACK FOOD	BAKING ITEMS	CANNED FOOD	VEGETABLES, FRUIT, UNPROCESSED FOOD
PET FOOD				
FROZEN FOOD				
MAGAZINES	CHECKOUT			FLOWERS GIFTS

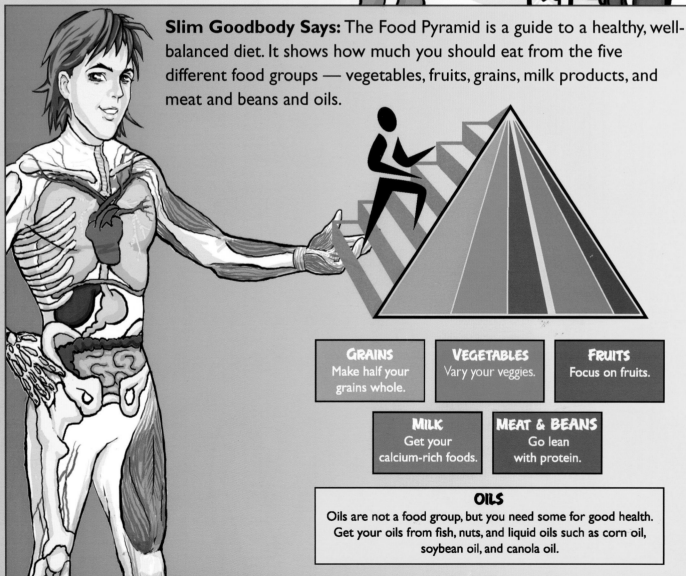

Slim Goodbody Says: The Food Pyramid is a guide to a healthy, well-balanced diet. It shows how much you should eat from the five different food groups — vegetables, fruits, grains, milk products, and meat and beans and oils.

GRAINS
Make half your grains whole.

VEGETABLES
Vary your veggies.

FRUITS
Focus on fruits.

MILK
Get your calcium-rich foods.

MEAT & BEANS
Go lean with protein.

OILS
Oils are not a food group, but you need some for good health. Get your oils from fish, nuts, and liquid oils such as corn oil, soybean oil, and canola oil.

asked, "So if you want to be healthy and buy **nutritious** foods, you should stick to the outer part of the store?"

"Some healthy foods like frozen fruits and vegetables, beans, and **whole-grain** cereals are stocked in the inner aisles. But so are the **processed foods** — like frozen pizzas or potato chips — that are less healthy. When I go shopping, I start with the outer part of the store where the most natural, healthier foods are. That way, I'm not as tempted to buy junk food from the inner aisles," explained Ethan.

We continued our tour and passed a big display of chocolate-frosted cookies at the end of the aisle. "Those look good. Are they on sale?" I asked.

"That's the oldest trick in the book. The store manager wants to make sure certain items sell. She tells us what to put on the end of the aisle. When we set up cookie or candy displays, people often buy the products shown. They think they're getting a better deal even if the products on the displays costs the same as the products in the inner aisles," explained Ethan.

TRICKS FOR TREATS

THE CHECKOUT TRAP

Finally, we came to the checkout lane. I hadn't eaten since lunch. But before I could reach for a candy bar, Ethan said, "People buy this junk food as they're checking out because they're usually tired and hungry. If I ever become the manager of this store, I'm going to make a lot of changes. I'll put healthy snacks in the checkout aisles and fruits and vegetables on our displays. People need to take care of their bodies and eat healthy foods. I really want to teach our customers about making healthy choices when they shop."

Slim Goodbody Says: Use these tips to be a smart shopper
• Plan ahead. Make a shopping list of healthy foods, and stick to it. You won't be as tempted to buy junk food at the store.
• Never go grocery shopping on an empty stomach. It is harder to avoid buying junk food when you are hungry.

Oils Can Foil a Healthy Diet

When I came to work the next day, Ethan asked me to stock bags of potato chips on the shelves. While I worked, I watched people shopping around me. I noticed that Ethan was right. The middle aisles were full of all sorts of unhealthy foods, and the shoppers were piling them into their carts.

After a while, Ethan came to check up on me.

"I never realized how many people eat potato chips and drink soda!" I said.

"Now you understand why I want to teach our customers about buying nutritious foods," said Ethan, shaking his head.

The Horrors of Hydrogenated Oil

"Well, butter is considered **hydrogenated** oil. Hydrogenated oils are processed and stay solid at room temperature. They're made out of animal fats and vegetable oils. They're full of **saturated fats** and sometimes **trans fats**. Both these fats are bad for your heart. They clog your arteries, narrowing them. This makes your heart work harder at pumping blood through your body," Ethan explained.

"I sure do. Aren't foods cooked in oils really bad for you?" I asked.

"They can be. The Food Pyramid is a guide that shows you how much you should eat from the different food groups. It says that you are supposed to eat some oils, but you should choose your oils carefully," explained Ethan.

"You mean some oils are healthier than others?" I asked.

"That's right. Cooking with olive, canola, or corn oil is healthier than cooking with butter," said Ethan.

"Why?" I asked.

"My mom always bakes with **lard** or shortening. Are those hydrogenated oils too?" I asked.

"I'm afraid so. The best way to get healthy oil in your diet is to eat nuts, avocados, and fish like salmon. These foods provide the healthiest oils," said Ethan.

"Cool, I love avocados!" I said happily.

Slim Goodbody Says: Compare these two lists of ingredients. Do you see hydrogenated oils in the ingredients? Which food do you think is healthier, Frosted Fruit and Oatmeal Toaster Treats or Fruit and Oatmeal Frosted Toastables?

Frosted Fruit and Oatmeal Toaster Treats

Wheat flour, sugar, high fructose corn syrup, partially hydrogenated soybean oil, oats, water, fructose, apple puree concentrate, dextrose, food starch modified, glycerin, tri calcium phosphate, raspberries, salt, milk, egg whites, natural and artificial flavor(s), datem, malic acid, niacin, sodium bicarbonate, gelatin, citric acid, thiamine mononitrate, riboflavin, artificial color, folic acid

Fruit and Oatmeal Frosted Toastables

Water, fructose, strawberries (strawberries, strawberry puree, sugar, concentrated boysenberry juice (for color), beet juice concentrate (for color), pectin, guar gum, locust bean gum, citric acid, natural flavor, turmeric (for color).

The earlier an ingredient appears in the list, the more of it is used in the food. Hydrogenated oils are the fourth ingredient in the Frosted Fruit and Oatmeal Toaster Treats! The Fruit and Oatmeal Frosted Toastables don't contain any hydrogenated oils, so this product is the smarter choice. Take care of your heart by choosing snacks without hydrogenated oils!

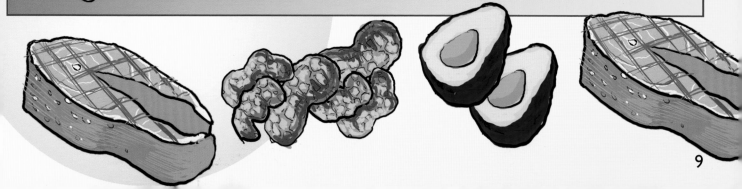

POSTERS AND PROTEIN

The next day, I was stacking cans of beans when Ethan came to see how I was doing. "I really like your idea of helping customers learn how to buy healthier foods," I told him. "Why don't we make posters about nutrition to help remind them to make healthy choices when they shop?"

"That's a fantastic idea, Mandy!" said Ethan. "We can make posters about each of the different food groups in the Food Pyramid. We could include information about how to choose the healthiest foods. We could put copies of specific food group posters wherever those items are sold."

FROM CHICKEN TO CHICKPEAS

I looked at the can of chickpeas in my hand. "Which food group are these in?" I asked.

"Chickpeas are a type of bean. Beans are part of the meat food group. Seeds, nuts, fish, eggs, and, of course, red meat and poultry are too. Foods from the meat and bean group are found all over the grocery store, from the beans and hard-boiled eggs in the salad bar to the fish and seafood counter," explained Ethan. "We could put a meat and beans food group poster wherever customers can buy those foods. Our posters could offer tips on how to choose healthy foods from the meat and beans group."

Slim Goodbody Says: The meat and beans food group offers **protein**, which builds your bones, muscles, **cartilage**, skin, and blood. If you eat all of the different foods in the meat and beans group, you will also get B vitamins, vitamin E, and minerals such as **iron, zinc, and magnesium**. Unfortunately, most people only eat red meat and poultry from this food group and miss out on some of these important vitamins and minerals.

Ethan helped me finish stacking the cans before we went back to the office. We found a big piece of paper, and I began to draw.

THE MEAT AND BEANS FOOD GROUP

Includes Seeds, Nuts, Fish, Eggs, Soy Products, Red Meat, and Poultry

Go Lean on Protein!

Choose lean meats and poultry. Remember processed deli meat can be high in unhealthy fat and sodium.

Mix Up Your Meats!

Try all of the foods in the meat and beans food group, including fish, beans, peas, nuts, and seeds.

Feast on Fresh Fish!

Fish like salmon, herring, sardines, and tuna are full of brain-building **omega-3 fats**. If you buy canned fish, make sure it is packed in water, not fattening oil.

GLORIOUS GRAINS

When I finished the poster, Ethan was amazed. "Step aside, Leonardo DaVinci! I didn't know that you were an artist! Do you think we can make a poster for the grains food group too?"

"That sounds great to me!" I said happily.

"OK. The grain poster should show the different foods in the grain food group. You'll need to include wheat, rice, oats, corn, and barley. But you also need to show foods made from those grains like bread, cereal, pasta, and tortillas," said Ethan.

"Ok, sure. So what are some tips we can share with our customers about choosing healthy grains?" I asked.

WHOLE GRAINS AHEAD

"Well, we should definitely tell them that whole grains, like whole-wheat bread and brown rice, are healthier than **refined** grains like white bread and white rice. Whole grains have more **fiber**, which helps with **digestion**," explained Ethan.

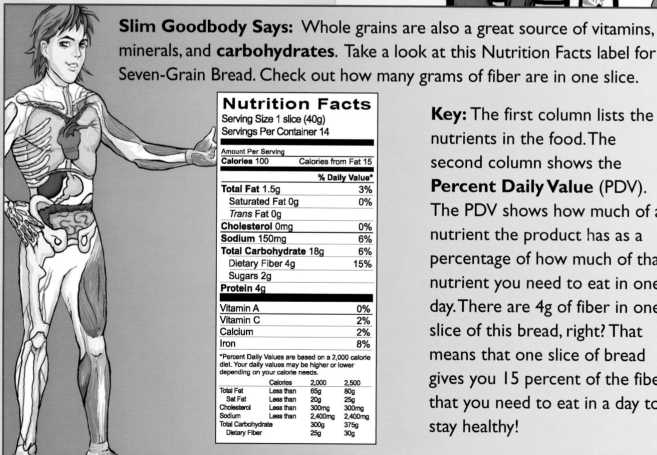

Slim Goodbody Says: Whole grains are also a great source of vitamins, minerals, and **carbohydrates**. Take a look at this Nutrition Facts label for Seven-Grain Bread. Check out how many grams of fiber are in one slice.

Nutrition Facts

Serving Size 1 slice (40g)
Servings Per Container 14

Amount Per Serving

Calories 100	Calories from Fat 15

	% Daily Value*
Total Fat 1.5g	3%
Saturated Fat 0g	0%
Trans Fat 0g	
Cholesterol 0mg	0%
Sodium 150mg	6%
Total Carbohydrate 18g	6%
Dietary Fiber 4g	15%
Sugars 2g	
Protein 4g	

Vitamin A	0%
Vitamin C	2%
Calcium	2%
Iron	8%

*Percent Daily Values are based on a 2,000 calorie diet. Your daily values may be higher or lower depending on your calorie needs.

	Calories	2,000	2,500
Total Fat	Less than	65g	80g
Sat Fat	Less than	20g	25g
Cholesterol	Less than	300mg	300mg
Sodium	Less than	2,400mg	2,400mg
Total Carbohydrate		300g	375g
Dietary Fiber		25g	30g

Key: The first column lists the nutrients in the food. The second column shows the **Percent Daily Value** (PDV). The PDV shows how much of a nutrient the product has as a percentage of how much of that nutrient you need to eat in one day. There are 4g of fiber in one slice of this bread, right? That means that one slice of bread gives you 15 percent of the fiber that you need to eat in a day to stay healthy!

"How are our customers supposed to know if the food they buy is made with whole grains?" I asked.

"They just need to look at the ingredients list on the back of the package. If whole grains are listed as one of the first ingredients, the customers will know it is a healthy choice," explained Ethan.

I began working on my poster.

THE GRAIN FOOD GROUP
Includes Wheat, Rice, Oats, Corn, Barley, Bread, Cereal, Tortillas, and Pasta

Try to make half of your grains whole!
The more whole grains you eat, the healthier you will be. Use the ingredients list on the back of the package to make sure the foods you buy are made with whole grains.

Don't be fooled!
Enriched flour is just another way of saying refined, white flour. White flour does not have as many vitamins and minerals as whole-grain wheat flour.

Look high and low!
You might have to go for a whole grains hunt! Companies sometimes pay grocery store to put their products at eye level or in places where the customer is bound to notice them. Less healthy grains like sugary cereals, fattening macaroni and cheese, or white bread are often at eye height. Companies think those items are more appealing and that their placement will make you grab them from the shelves.

MIGHTY MILK

The next week, Ethan found me bagging groceries. "I've got great news!" he said with a grin. "The customers love your posters! They've been commenting on your artwork, and they like the tips on choosing healthy foods."

"Cool!" I said.

"And that's not all! I've been promoted to manager. Now we can really make some changes around here," declared Ethan.

"Congratulations, Ethan!"

"The first thing we need to do is design a poster for the milk food group," Ethan said as we made our way back to the office. There, we planned our next poster.

"OK. So milk, cheese, yogurt, and ice cream are all in the milk food group, right?" I asked.

"Right. But some things made from milk, like cream cheese, cream, and butter, lose their **calcium** when they're being made. They aren't considered part of the milk food group," explained Ethan.

MILK'S MARVELOUS MINERALS

"OK. Everyone knows that calcium builds and strengthens your bones and teeth. Are there other healthy minerals in the milk food group?" I asked.

"**Potassium** is great for your heart, muscles, and kidneys," said Ethan. "The problem is that a lot of milk products also are high in fat. We need to help customers choose healthy, low-fat dairy products."

14

Slim Goodbody Says: Compare the Nutrition Facts labels for these two kinds of milk. Which one do you think is healthier?

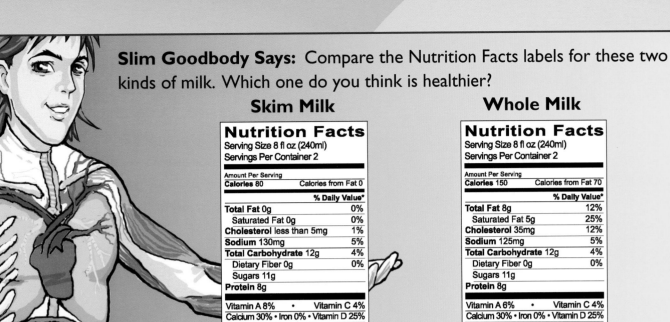

Skim Milk

Nutrition Facts
Serving Size 8 fl oz (240ml)
Servings Per Container 2

Amount Per Serving	
Calories 80	Calories from Fat 0

	% Daily Value*
Total Fat 0g	0%
Saturated Fat 0g	0%
Cholesterol less than 5mg	1%
Sodium 130mg	5%
Total Carbohydrate 12g	4%
Dietary Fiber 0g	0%
Sugars 11g	
Protein 8g	

Vitamin A 8%	•	Vitamin C 4%
Calcium 30% • Iron 0% • Vitamin D 25%		

*Percent Daily Values are based on a 2,000 calorie diet. Your daily values may be higher or lower depending on your calorie needs.

	Calories	2,000	2,500
Total Fat	Less than	65g	80g
Sat Fat	Less than	20g	25g
Cholesterol	Less than	300mg	300mg
Sodium	Less than	2,400mg	2,400mg
Total Carbohydrate		300g	375g
Dietary Fiber		25g	30g

Whole Milk

Nutrition Facts
Serving Size 8 fl oz (240ml)
Servings Per Container 2

Amount Per Serving	
Calories 150	Calories from Fat 70

	% Daily Value*
Total Fat 8g	12%
Saturated Fat 5g	25%
Cholesterol 35mg	12%
Sodium 125mg	5%
Total Carbohydrate 12g	4%
Dietary Fiber 0g	0%
Sugars 11g	
Protein 8g	

Vitamin A 6%	•	Vitamin C 4%
Calcium 30% • Iron 0% • Vitamin D 25%		

*Percent Daily Values are based on a 2,000 calorie diet. Your daily values may be higher or lower depending on your calorie needs.

	Calories	2,000	2,500
Total Fat	Less than	65g	80g
Sat Fat	Less than	20g	25g
Cholesterol	Less than	300mg	300mg
Sodium	Less than	2,400mg	2,400mg
Total Carbohydrate		300g	375g
Dietary Fiber		25g	30g

Answer: The whole milk is high in saturated fat, which is bad for your heart. The skim milk has no saturated fat and is still high in bone-building calcium.

"OK, here goes," I said, and began creating the Milk Food Group poster.

THE MILK FOOD GROUP
Includes Milk, Cheese, and Yogurt

Mighty Minerals:
Foods in the milk food group are full of important minerals like calcium and potassium.

Stay Away from Saturated Fats:
Many milk products are high in saturated fats, which are bad for your heart. Use the Nutrition Facts label to choose milk products that are heart healthy! Choose low fat (1 percent fat) or fat free (skim milk) when you choose milk, yogurt, and other milk products.

Lactose Intolerant?:
Many people can't digest a chemical in milk products called lactose. If they eat cheese or milk, they often feel sick. If you are lactose intolerant, get your calcium from foods with extra calcium. Choose juices with extra calcium, soy drinks, and leafy green vegetables.

TRICKS OF THE TRADE: FOOD ADVERTISING

When I got home, I found my mother making dinner in the kitchen.

"How was work?" she asked.

"Awesome. You were right, Mom. I really am learning a lot about nutrition. And Ethan told me today that the customers love my food group posters. I think we really can teach people how to choose healthy foods when they shop," I told her.

"I love hearing that you are using your artistic skills at work and that you're trying to educate the public about eating healthy foods. Unfortunately, you are up against many food companies that pay millions of dollars for **advertising** to convince people to buy junk food," said my mother with a sigh.

"I never thought about that," I said.

THE MEAT AND BEANS FOOD GROUP
Includes Seeds, Nuts, Fish, Eggs, Soy Pro...
Red Meat, and Poultry

Go Lean on Protein
Choose lean meats and poultry. Remem...
meat can be high in unhealthy...

Mix Up Yo...
Try all of the foods in the mea...
including fish, beans, pe...

Feast...
Fish...

THE GRAIN FOOD GRO...
Includes Wheat, Rice, Oats, Corn, Barle...
Cereal, Tortillas, and Pasta

Try to make half of your g...
The more whole grains you eat, the heal...
the ingredients list on the back of the pa...
foods you buy are made with...

Don't be fo...
Enriched flour is just another way...
White flour does not have as m...
whole-grain...

Look hi...
You might have to go for a...
sometimes pay grocery st...
or in places where the c...
healthy grains like suga...
or white bread are often...
items are more appealing and th...
grab them from the shelves.

THE MILK FOOD GROUP
Includes Milk, Cheese, and Yogurt

Foods in the milk food group are full of important minerals like calcium and potassium.

Mighty Minerals:

Stay Away from Saturated Fats:
Many milk products are high in saturated fats, which are bad for your heart. Use the Nutrition Facts label to choose milk products that are heart healthy! Choose low fat (1 percent fat) or fat free (skim milk) when you choose milk, yogurt, and other milk products.

Lactose Intolerant?:
Many people can't digest a chemical in milk products called lactose. If they eat...
are lactose...
calcium...
milk, they often feel sick. If you...
calcium from foods with extra...
calcium, soy drinks, and leafy...
...les.

ADVERTISING'S INFLUENCE

"Just think about the ads you see on TV. Advertisers use all sorts of tricks to catch kids' attention," said my mother. "Cartoon characters make it seem like eating sugary cereals is fun. Companies put free toys in a package of cereal to make people want to buy it. Or they use slogans like 'low fat' or 'fat free' to make their product sound healthy to parents and other adults, even if it isn't."

"I always see pro athletes and supermodels selling things on TV. They make it seem glamorous and cool to eat a certain kind of food," I told her.

My mother nodded and added, "And those stars are paid a lot of money to say good things about a product even if they don't like it."

"Wow, I guess we're going to have to do a lot more than make a few posters to get our customers to make healthy decisions," I said.

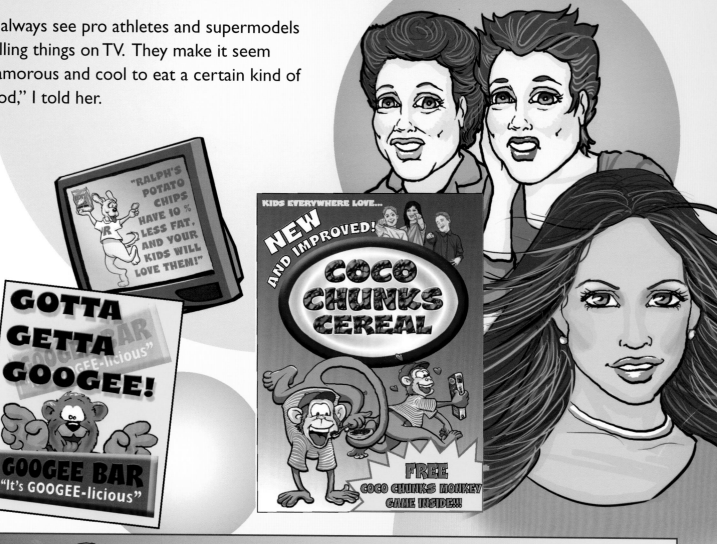

Slim Goodbody Says: Next time you see a food advertisement, look for the tricks advertisers use to make you want their product. Figure out how the ad tries to appeal to you. Do they make you want to go out and buy unhealthy food? Where do you see advertisements — on TV, the Internet, or billboards?

Fabulous Fruits

The next day, I arrived at work early. I found Ethan in the produce section. "Ethan, we're going to have to do a lot more than put up posters if we are going to influence what people buy," I said firmly.

"I know, we're just getting started. Today, we're going to make a big fruit display. It should include everything in the fruit food group. The fruits can be fresh, frozen, canned, dried, or 100 percent juice. Do you think you can create a fruit sculpture?" asked Ethan.

"That sounds like a great idea! We can have information about the different vitamins and minerals you get from eating fruits too," I suggested.

Fruit Facts

"Yeah! We should also have a poster that encourages people to eat different kinds and colors of fruits. The more kinds and colors of fruits they eat, the more nutrients they'll get," said Ethan.

"So the poster should include fruits like pink grapefruits, blue blueberries, red apples, yellow bananas, and green kiwis?" I asked.

"Sounds good! And brown figs, orange nectarines, and purple grapes! We should also advertise the fruits and vegetables that are in season and grown locally. Fruits and vegetables cost less when they're in season, and they taste better too," Ethan told me.

Ethan and I got to work on our fruit sculpture.

Slim Goodbody Says: Fruits provide important vitamins, minerals, carbohydrates, and fiber. Vitamin C is in many different kinds of fruit, especially kiwi, oranges, strawberries, and cantaloupes. It helps heal cuts and wounds and keeps your teeth and gums healthy.

A Fruit-Eating Figure

Then I thought about some of the food advertisers' tricks I had seen on TV. "We should include a big cutout of a friendly, fruit-eating cartoon character," I said. "It might catch kids' attention and make them want to eat the fruit too. What about Paula the Panda Bear?".

"Sounds great to me!" said Ethan. "We could even dress you up as Paula the Panda Bear and have you help kids choose different fruits," Ethan laughed and winked at me. "Just kidding!"

After finishing the Panda Bear cutout, I put it at the top of the fruit sculpture.

"It's a masterpiece!" I exclaimed with pride.

Customers began to notice the fruit sculpture and came closer to see what it was. "Buy our delicious fruit! It tastes great, and it's good for you too," I said happily.

Slim Goodbody Says: Fruits contain fiber, which helps you feel full. Most fruits are naturally low in fat, sodium, and calories. None have cholesterol.

THE VALUE OF VEGETABLES

Over the next week, we were amazed to see how many people were buying fruit.

"This is incredible!" said Ethan. "I guess Paula the Panda Bear really is catching people's attention. The only problem is that our customers still aren't buying many vegetables. What should we do?" asked Ethan.

"Well, sometimes food advertisers pay a **spokesperson** like a famous athlete or model to talk about a product and how delicious it is. Advertisers want people to think they will be more attractive or popular if they buy a product," I told him.

"That's a great idea. Roger Nash, the pitcher for our local baseball team, is always on TV telling kids to eat healthy foods. Maybe he would come in and talk with people about eating vegetables," suggested Ethan.

"Perfect!" I said.

A VOICE FOR VEGGIES

A couple of weeks later, Roger Nash stood in the vegetable section, surrounded by carrots, broccoli, spinach, and corn. Wearing his uniform and a sparkling smile, he handed out autographs and told shoppers about the importance of eating vegetables.

"Vegetables and vegetable juice have all sorts of vitamins, minerals, carbohydrates, and fiber. Can anyone give me examples of the vitamins and minerals in vegetables?" he asked the crowd.

One girl raised her hand and suggested, "Dark green vegetables, like broccoli, spinach, and dark green lettuce, have a lot of calcium. It keeps your bones and teeth strong,"

"That's right!" said Roger.

Another child raised his hand. "Orange vegetables, like sweet potatoes and carrots, have vitamin A. It keeps your skin and eyes healthy and helps fight off **infections** too."

"Exactly! Unfortunately, most people across the United States don't eat enough vegetables," said Roger.

Roger held up two cans of soup. "To choose healthy foods, you can use the Nutrition Facts labels. This Nutrition Facts label shows that this soup has 50 percent of the recommended daily value of vitamin A. That means that it has half the vitamin A you need in a day!"

Slim Goodbody Says: Soups can be a great source of vegetables and nutrients but they can also contain a lot of sodium, or salt. Too much sodium can lead to high blood pressure. Use these Nutrition Facts labels to decide which of these soups has less sodium (salt) per serving. Why do you think that the "healthy" soup has a little more fat?

"Healthy" Vegetable Soup

Nutrition Facts
Serving Size 1 cup (245g)
Servings Per Container 2

Amount Per Serving	
Calories 90	Calories from Fat 9

	% Daily Value*
Total Fat 1g	2%
Saturated Fat 0g	0%
Trans Fat 0g	
Cholesterol 5mg	2%
Sodium 440mg	18%
Total Carbohydrates 16g	5%
Dietary Fiber 2g	8%
Sugars 5g	
Protein 3g	

Vitamin A 50%	•	Vitamin C 2%	
Calcium 2%	•	Iron 4%	

*Percent Daily Values are based on a 2,000 calorie diet. Your daily values may be higher or lower depending on your calorie needs.

Traditional Vegetable Soup

Nutrition Facts
Serving Size 1 cup (245g)
Servings Per Container 2

Amount Per Serving	
Calories 80	Calories from Fat 4

	% Daily Value*
Total Fat 0.5g	15.5278 in%
Saturated Fat 0g	0%
Trans Fat 0g	
Cholesterol 0mg	0%
Sodium 790mg	33%
Total Carbohydrates 16g	5%
Dietary Fiber 2g	8%
Sugars 7g	
Protein 3g	

Vitamin A 35%	•	Vitamin C 4%	
Calcium 2%	•	Iron 4%	

*Percent Daily Values are based on a 2,000 calorie diet. Your daily values may be higher or lower depending on your calorie needs.

Key: The "healthy" soup has less sodium but more fat. Both fat and salt bring out flavor, so if the amount of salt is lower, the amount of fat might be higher. The "healthy" soup is still low in fat and a good choice for a meal.

MAKING DECISIONS FOR A HEALTHY LIFE

For the next week, we offered one of Roger's autographed baseball cards to every person buying a fresh, frozen, dried, or canned vegetable.

"I think this is really working!" said Ethan, as we watched people pile vegetables into their shopping carts.

"I know! It really seems like shoppers are starting to make better decisions. I just wish I could convince myself to buy healthy foods," I sighed. "It is so hard to buy healthy snacks at break time when I can just go to the bakery section and buy a doughnut or cupcake."

DIRECTIONS FOR HEALTHY DECISIONS

"I know. It used to be hard for me too. Now I am so used to eating healthy foods, however, I don't even crave those sweets anymore. My dad taught me a great decision-making tool to help choose healthy foods," said Ethan. "First you *identify your choices* and then you *evaluate each choice and think about their consequences*. Next, you *identify the healthiest decision* and finally *take action*. Afterward, you *evaluate your decision* to decide if it was the right choice."

"That sounds like a lot of work just to decide on a snack," I thought. I decided to give it a try anyway.

ROGER NASH

Later, at break time, I identified my choices for a snack. "I can buy these carrot sticks from the vegetable section or a candy bar at the checkout aisle," I thought. "The candy bar tastes good, but it's high in fat. I never feel very good after I eat it. The carrots are good too, but they have vitamins and are low in fat. They're clearly the healthy choice," I said to myself. I took action by buying the carrot sticks.

After I finished my snack, I remembered Ethan's advice to evaluate my decision. "I'm not hungry anymore, and I feel good knowing that I ate a healthy snack. I guess I'd choose the carrot sticks again." I realized that it wasn't as hard to eat healthy foods when I took the time to think about my choices.

Slim Goodbody Says: Now it's your turn! Use Ethan's decision-making strategy to make healthy decisions about the foods you buy. The next time you are at the grocery store, will you choose whole-grain cereal or frosted chocolate flakes?

Remember:
• Identify your choices
• Evaluate each choice and think about their consequences
• Identify the healthiest decision
• Take action
• Evaluate your decision

Great Goals for Healthy Shopping

The next week, Ethan found me while I was on break. "Have you been buying healthier foods these days?" he asked.

"It's not as hard as I thought it would be. Sometimes though, I don't pay attention, and I wind up buying potato chips or cookies," I admitted.

"No one is perfect. It's OK to eat chips every once in a while. You know, sometimes it's easier to make healthy choices when you're working toward a goal. Maybe you should try setting a goal for yourself," suggested Ethan.

"I don't know a lot about **goal setting**. Do you have any more handy tools that might help?" I asked with a grin.

A Guide to Setting Great Goals!

"As a matter of fact, I do!" laughed Ethan. He found a piece of paper and pencil and gave them to me. "OK. Your first step is to *set a realistic goal and write it down.* It helps if you set a goal that can be accomplished in a specific amount of time, like two or three weeks. Then you *list the steps that you will need to take to reach your goal.* Next you *think about the support you'll need from friends and family.* Then you *evaluate your progress* and if you have reached your goal, you can *reward yourself.*"

"OK, I guess my goal is to buy healthy snacks at the grocery store for the next two weeks. I'll compare the Nutrition Facts labels and the ingredients lists on the snack packages to decide if a snack is healthy before I buy it," I told him.

My Goal: Buy Healthy Snacks For The Next Two Weeks.

"So do you need help from your friends or family to help you reach your goal?" asked Ethan.

"If you see me buying junk food, you can remind me of my goal," I suggested.

"I can do that. And if you reach your goal, how will you reward yourself?" asked Ethan.

"I don't know. I guess it's as important to have a healthy reward as it is to have a healthy goal. Maybe I'll buy myself some new art supplies for camp," I said.

"Sounds good!" said Ethan.

25

Get Active! Be an Advocate for Good Health!

After work, I went home and found my mother doing yard work. "Hey, mom! You won't believe it! I have a new goal to stop buying junk food," I said smiling.

"Wow, Mandy, I never thought I would hear you say those words," my mother laughed. "I guess you really have learned some important lessons at your new job,"

"It's true! And our customers are learning the same lessons. I was bagging groceries today, and I was amazed to see all of the fruits, vegetables, and whole-grain foods they were buying. I think Ethan and I have really made a difference."

An Agent for Change

"I am so proud of you, Mandy. You might not realize it, but you've become a health **advocate**," said my mother.

"What do you mean?" I asked.

"A health advocate is someone who works to make their family, school, and community healthier and stronger. Health advocates *take a healthy stand on an issue*. Then they work to *persuade others to make a healthy choice*. And most importantly they have to *be convincing*," explained my mother.

"Well, if you put it that way, I guess I am a health advocate. Ethan and I decided that we wanted to teach our customers about making healthy choices. We made posters and fruit sculptures to help persuade people to buy healthy foods. We were pretty convincing. We even had a baseball pitcher come in and talk to shoppers about the benefits of eating vegetables," I said.

"The world needs more people like you, Mandy!" said my mother.

Slim Goodbody Says: Now it's your turn! Does your family buy a lot of junk food at the grocery store? Maybe it is time to teach them about the importance of eating a well-balanced diet. Be a health advocate and use what you've learned about smart shopping from this book to help your friends and family buy healthy foods.

- Milk, yogurt, and cheese are great sources of bone-building calcium.
- Choose low- or no-fat milk and yogurt.
- Saturated fats are bad for your heart.
- Look on the Nutrition Facts label to make sure that your dairy products are low in saturated fats.

MILK

Low Fat Yogurt

- Steer clear of unhealthy hydrogenated oils
- Nuts, avocados, and oily fish like salmon contain the healthiest oils.

A Summary of Smart Shopping

After talking with my mother, I went upstairs to my room. Art camp was only a few weeks away, and I wanted to do some painting. I pulled out my paints and pinned a huge piece of stiff paper to my wall. I began to make a giant painting of everything that I'd learned while working at the grocery store. I wanted to thank Ethan for teaching me about nutrition. A painting might make a good gift. Maybe he would even hang it in the store!

IEST FOODS

- The more whole grains you can eat, the healthier you will be. Brown rice, whole-wheat bread, and rolled oats are full of fiber, which helps with digestion.

- The refined grains in white bread, pastries, and white rice are not as healthy as whole-grain foods, such as brown rice and whole-wheat bread.

- Fruits are full of vitamins. Vitamin C helps your body grow, heals cuts and wounds, and keeps teeth and gums healthy.

- Eat fruits of different colors. That way you'll make sure to get as many important vitamins as you can.

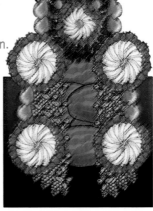

- Go lean on protein. Find the meats with the least amount of fat.

- Don't just eat red meat and poultry. Fish, beans, peas, nuts, and seeds are also in the meat and bean food group. They are important sources of vitamins and minerals like iron.

- Fish like salmon, herring, sardines, or tuna are full of brain-building omega-3 fats.

PAULA THE PANDA SAYS: EAT LOTS OF FRUIT!

- Dark green leafy vegetables are full of calcium, which makes you bones and teeth strong.

- Orange vegetables are full of Vitamin A, which fights off infections and keeps your eyes and skin healthy.

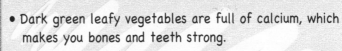

Slim Goodbody Says: Make your own mural representing what you learned from reading this book. Hang it in your room to remind yourself to be a smart shopper!

Glossary

advertising The use of different kinds of media, including television, radio, the Internet, magazines, and newspapers, to promote a product or service

advocate A person who supports or speaks in favor of a cause or an idea

calcium A mineral your body needs to grow strong teeth and bones

carbohydrates The body's main energy source from foods. Most carbohydrates come from plants such as grains.

cartilage A strong, flexible material that makes up parts of the body, including the ears and nose

diabetes A condition in which people have too much sugar in their blood. People with diabetes cannot produce enough insulin, the substance the body needs to use sugar properly.

digestion The process of breaking down food so the body can use it

fiber Material in food that cannot be digested but helps with going to the bathroom

goal setting Making plans that will help you achieve something that you want to do

high blood pressure A condition that forces the heart to work harder to pump blood

hydrogenated Describes a liquid fat that has been chemically altered into a solid fat, such as butter or margarine

infections Sicknesses or diseases caused by germs

lard A soft white fat from a pig

nutrition The study of food and diet

nutritious Describing foods that give the body energy and help it grow and heal

omega-3 fats Types of fats found in foods such as walnuts, some fruits and vegetables, and coldwater fish such as herring, mackerel, sturgeon, and anchovies. Omega-3 fats help reduce the risk of heart disease and other health problems.

Percent Daily Value A section of the Nutrition Facts label that shows the amount of each nutrient in a serving of a food. It is usually based on a 2,000-calorie diet.

processed foods Foods that have been altered or changed from their original, natural form to last longer or look or taste different. Processed foods often contain unhealthy ingredients like added sweeteners and preservatives to keep them from spoiling.

refined Describing a food that has had its nutritious parts removed

saturated fats Type of fats that usually come from animal products such as meat and dairy products. Saturated fats are solid at room temperature.

spokesperson A famous person who is paid to say positive things about a product

trans fats Forms of fats found in solid fats, such as stick margarine and vegetable shortening, and in some processed foods. Trans fats improve the flavor and texture of foods, but they increase the risk of heart disease.

whole-grain Describes a product that contains all edible parts of the grain, including the bran, germ, and endosperm.

FOR MORE INFORMATION

Fruits and Veggies: More Matters

www.fruitsandveggiesmatter.gov

Find out how many fruits and vegetables you need and try out healthy recipes.

Nutrition Explorations

www.nutritionexplorations.org/kids/main.asp

Play games, learn more about the Food Pyramid, and hear why it's important to eat right.

PBS Go Kids: Don't Buy It—Get Media Smart—Buying Smart

pbskids.org/dontbuyit/buyingsmart

Discover more about reading advertisements and becoming a smart shopper.

United States Department of Agriculture: My Pyramid Animated

www.mypyramid.gov/global_nav/media_animation.html

View a fun, animated explanation of the Food Pyramid and the different food groups.

United States Department of Agriculture: MyPyramid for Kids

www.mypyramid.gov/kids

Find information on the Food Pyramid, track you own intake of food, and play nutrition games!

INDEX

ABOUT THE AUTHOR

John Burstein (also known as Slim Goodbody) has been entertaining and educating children for over thirty years. His programs have been broadcast on CBS, PBS, Nickelodeon, USA, and Discovery. He has won numerous awards including the Parent's Choice Award and the President's Council's Fitness Leader Award. Currently, Mr. Burstein tours the country with his live multimedia show "Bodyology." For more information, please visit slimgoodbody.com